Vegan Candy and Chocolate Bar Cookbook

How To Make Vegan Candy and Chocolate Bar

DEDICATION

Contents

Vegan Peanut Butter Cups

So easy to make and they taste just like Reese's! A great recipe for Easter, Christmas, or just when you are craving chocolate.

Prep Time: 15 mins

Cook Time: 5 mins

Total Time: 20 mins

Course: Dessert

Cuisine: American, Canadian

Servings: 12 (around 10 - 12 large peanut butter cups, or around 20 small cups)

Calories: 101kcal

Ingredients

½ cup natural peanut butter (or any other kind of nut butter you like!)

¼ cup powdered sugar

½ teaspoon vanilla extract

¼ teaspoon salt

1 ¼ cups vegan chocolate chips

US Customary - Metric

To make Vegan Peanut Butter Cups, just mix up the peanut butter with powdered sugar, vanilla extract, and salt. It forms this kind of peanut butter dough. Taste it. You're welcome.

Melt your chocolate chips in a double boiler, then remove from heat. If your chocolate firms up while you are working with it, just pop it back on the double boiler to melt again.

If you don't have a double boiler, you can use my method, and just pop a heat safe bowl over a pot of boiling water. Congratulations, you just made yourself a double boiler.

The reason you want to melt the chips in a double boiler vs. a pot directly on the heat, is that chocolate burns and turns grainy very easily, and once it burns there is no going back. Your chocolate is ruined. So melting it in a double boiler ensures it doesn't burn.

You could also melt your chips in a microwave, but I don't have one of those, so you are on your own with that one.

Take some cupcake liners and pour in about 1 to 2 teaspoons of chocolate. Just enough to cover the bottom of the liner. You can use the spoon to spread the chocolate around.

Now pinch off some of your peanut butter dough, and shape into a disc that is just a bit smaller than your liner, so that there is room for the chocolate to go around the edges of the dough. This does not have to be beautiful.

Now use another spoonful or two of chocolate to cover the peanut butter disc. You may need to use your spoon to help spread the chocolate. Repeat with all of the remaining chocolate and peanut butter dough.

Put the chocolates on a baking tray so they are easier to manage, and then pop them in the fridge for about 30 minutes, until the chocolate has completely firmed up and set.

Once set you can peel off the cupcake liners, or just trim down the wrappers if you want to leave them on. Store in an airtight container in the cupboard.

You can also use any chocolate mold or silicon mold to make fun shapes.

Or if you are feeling crafty, you can also shape the peanut butter dough into balls or egg shapes and then just dip the dough into the chocolate and lay on parchment paper to set.

Vegan Chocolate Caramels

Rich & gooey homemade vegan chocolate caramels. So decadent &

delicious and surprisingly easy to make. Perfect as an indulgent treat or as a gift for someone special.

PREP TIME: 30 mins

COOK TIME: 5 mins

TOTAL TIME: 35 mins

COURSE: Candy, Dessert

CUISINE: vegan

SERVINGS: 35 small chocolates

CALORIES: 73 kcal

INGREDIENTS

1 chocolate mold

½ cup / 100 g coconut sugar

2 tablespoons water

2 tablespoons tahini , or any other nut butter

2 tablespoons coconut oil (refined or unrefined is fine)

¼ teaspoon fine salt

½ teaspoon vanilla extract

2 cups / 300 g vegan dark chocolate

INSTRUCTIONS

Add the coconut sugar and the water to a pan. Place over a medium heat and cook until the sugar has completely dissolved and it is just starting to bubble. DO NOT STIR!! If you need to, just swirl the pan a bit. It will take 2- 3 minutes max. Do not leave it unattended as it will burn very easily if left too long.

Remove from the heat and add the coconut oil, tahini, salt and vanilla. Stir very well until it is all well combined. It is normal to see a few light flecks through it. If you have trouble getting it to come together put it over a very low heat again for 30 seconds or so.

Remove from the heat and leave to cool. It will be very runny at first but will thicken up nicely as it cools.

When the caramel is cool melt your chocolate. I melt mine in a bowl over a pan of gently simmering water.

Spoon some melted chocolate into the bottom of each mold. I used a spoon and a knife to just push the melted chocolate gently off the edge of it into the molds. You need a depth of about 3-4 mms. No need to be too exact. Just eyeball it. Remember though if it's too thin the will be very hard to remove from the mold intact.

Once you have chocolate in each mold use the end of a knife to just push the chocolate pooled in the bottom up the sides of each mold to coat it. Make sure it's quite thick so that they don't end up too fragile once set.

Now spoon some caramel into each mold. You need to leave room for about 2-3mm of chocolate to be poured on the top. Don't be tempted to overdo it as you'll end up with a gooey mess. The caramel will level itself out as you pour it in.

Now cover the caramel with some more chocolate and use a pallet knife or the back of a regular knife to run along the top and level everything off nicely.

Pop the mold into the freezer. Make sure it is kept flat. Within 20-30 minutes they will be hard enough to turn out of the mold.

If you only have one mold you will need to repeat the process. Your chocolate should still be melted enough to continue but if it isn't just warm it slightly again.

NOTES

Store your chocolate caramels in a sealed container in the fridge. They will keep well for a couple of weeks.

If you have any caramel left it keeps well in the fridge and will turn liquid again if warmed gently. It's great served with ice-cream, waffles , pancakes , popcorn and baked bananas.

Healthy Gummy Fruit Snacks

Agar is the key ingredient that makes these Healthy Gummy Fruit Snacks into solid form. It's like voo-doo witchcraft. Do note that though agar plays as a great substitute for gelatin, it doesn't always give the same texture. These aren't chewy like you find with Gummy Bears but are still tasty and pose as a great snack option for your kids!

INGREDIENTS

STRAWBERRY GUMMIES:

1/2 c. strawberries

3/4 c. apple juice (or water)

1–3 Tbsp. maple syrup

juice of lemon wedge

1 1/2 Tbsp. agar powder (or 3 Tbsp. agar flakes)

BLUEBERRY GUMMIES:

1/2 c. blueberries

3/4 c. apple juice (or water)

1–3 Tbsp. maple syrup

juice of a lemon wedge

1 1/2 Tbsp. agar powder (or 3 Tbsp. agar flakes)

KIWI SPINACH GUMMIES:

2 kiwis, peeled and chopped

1 c. spinach

3/4 c. apple juice (or water)

1–3 Tbsp. maple syrup

1 1/2 Tbsp. agar powder (or 3 Tbsp. agar flakes)

juice of a lemon wedge

ORANGE GUMMIES:

1 small orange, peeled

1/2 c. orange juice

1–2 Tbsp. maple syrup

1 1/2 Tbsp. agar powder (or 3 Tbsp. agar flakes)

juice of a lemon wedge

INSTRUCTIONS

Blend together the fruit, apple juice or water, and 1 Tbsp. of maple syrup (if using apple juice) or 2-3 Tbsp. if using water, together until smooth.

Place into a saucepan and bring to a boil.

Stir in the agar powder and reduce to a simmer for 2 minutes. The agar should be completely dissolved by now. Add the lemon juice and mix. Add more maple syrup if needed at this point.

Pour into desired molds (I used this one) and refrigerate until sets (approximately 30 minutes). If you do not have any fun molds, fear not. Simply line an 8×8 pan with parchment paper and pour the mix into the pan. Allow to set, remove from the pan and slice into small rectangles.

Keep chilled in the fridge for up to 1 week in an airtight container.

NUTRITION

Serving Size: 5 Fruit Snacks

Calories: 30

Sugar: 5g

Sodium: 0mg

Fat: 0g

Carbohydrates: 7.5g

Rose Turkish Delight, Vegan Gluten Free

Prep Time

10 mins

Cook Time

1 hr 15 mins

Total Time

1 hr 25 mins

Although this recipe may seem complicated at first, once you read through it a couple of times and organize your ingredients and supplies, it simple enough. You will be rewarded with sugared pillows of rose petal confection. Placed in a small tin and tied with a satin bow it is an un-forgettable gift.

Course: Dessert

Cuisine: Turkish

Servings: 10 people

Mediavine

Ingredients

3 1/4 cups water

4 1/2 cups granulated sugar

3/4 tsp cream of tartar

3 tsp lemon zest

2 tbsp lemon juice

1 cup corn starch

3 tsp rose water

2-3 drops pink food coloring if desired

1 cup powdered sugar (for dusting)

1 cup Pistachios or any chopped nuts

Instructions

First off guys, this is candy. Candy is a petulant creature, humidity and altitude can significantly affect the texture of any candy. Try making meringues on a rainy day and you'll understand what I mean. So understand that once in a while a tried and true candy recipe fails for no discernible reason. Them's the risks.

Secondly you will be working with hot syrup. A burn from hot sugar syrup is serious, pay attention and save that glass of wine to drink while the candy is setting. Thank you for listening

Line your tin or mold with oiled plastic wrap allowing, the extra to hang over the sides. I used a square 8X8" cookie tin.

In a medium sized sauce pan, over medium heat, bring your sugar, 2 cups of the listed water, lemon juice and zest to a boil. Whisk until sugar is dissolved. Reduce your heat to medium low and keep the mixture at a simmer. Stir every few minutes with a wooden or silicone spoon. Clip your candy thermometer to the side of the pan and check until your syrup reaches 240 F (115 C).

Meanwhile while your sugar syrup is cooking.

In another saucepan whisk together remaining water, cornstarch and cream of tarter over medium heat. Whisk your corn starch mixture until it comes to boil. Really put your back into the whisking because there should be no lumps.

If you look into the pot and think "Oh crap, a giant blew his nose right into the pot while my back was turned" then you have the correct consistency.

When your sugar syrup just reaches 240°F(115°C) pour your syrup into the cornstarch mixture bit by bit. Stir well after each addition until all the syrup is incorporated into the cornstarch. Whisk like the devil until the two mixtures are fully incorporated.

Turn on a good podcast or invite a friend over for coffee. You are now a servant to the Turkish delight recipe. For one hour you will need to thoroughly stir the pot every 2-3 minutes. Keep the mixture on super low heat the whole time.

After an hour passes remove from the heat. Stir in the rose water with the correct food coloring if needed to heighten the color. This would be the time to add the nuts.

Pour the viscous mixture into your mold. Leave out on counter until firm. 10-12 hours.

Do Not Place In Fridge! Do Not Place In Fridge! Do Not Place In Fridge!

Once firm, remove from the mold and cut into squares. Toss your squares in confectioners sugar.

Your turkish delight will last a week or maybe two.

Vegan Peppermint Patties

Soft, creamy, sweet, minty filling, surrounded by luscious chocolate. One of the dessert worlds best combos in my opinion. Only 5 easy ingredients to make vegan peppermint patties (no really, that's it). They make a great gift (if you are ok with giving them away). They also store for a long time in the fridge or freezer making them a great little sweet treat to have on hand.

Prep Time: 25 mins

Cook Time: 10 mins

Total Time: 35 mins

Course: Dessert

Cuisine: American, Canadian

Servings: 24 patties

Calories: 136kcal

Ingredients

3 cups powdered sugar

¼ cup vegan butter

¼ cup agave (use light coloured agave to keep the filling white)

1 teaspoon peppermint extract

1 ½ cups vegan chocolate chips

US Customary - Metric

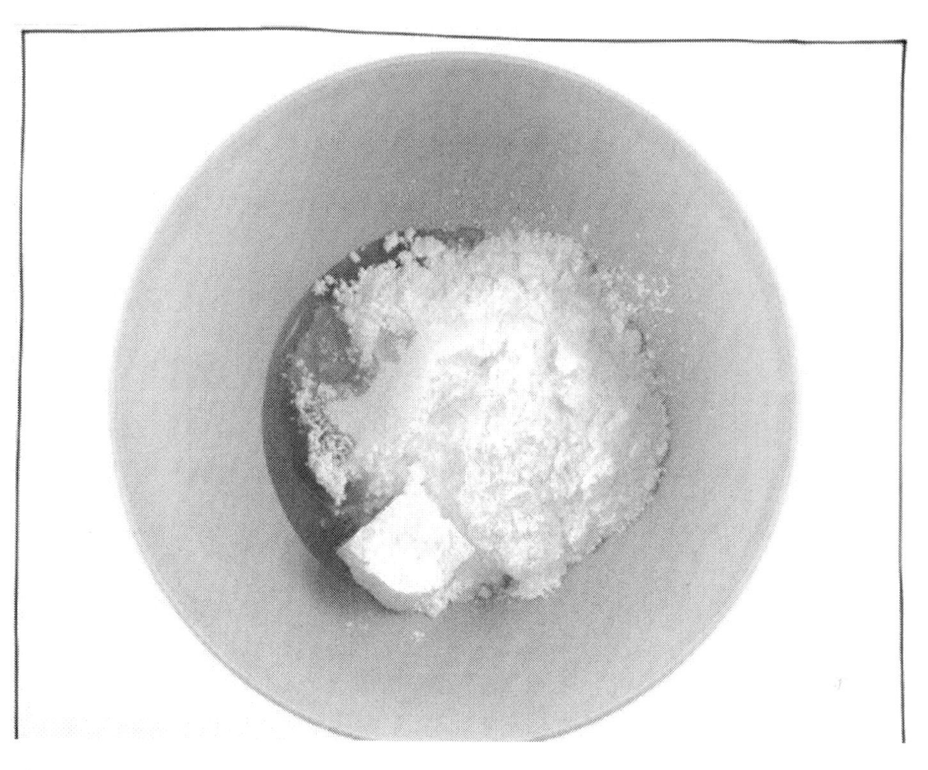

To make Vegan Peppermint Patties: use a hand mixer or stand mixer with a large bowl to beat the powdered sugar, vegan butter, agave, and peppermint extract together, making sure the butter gets completely mixed it.

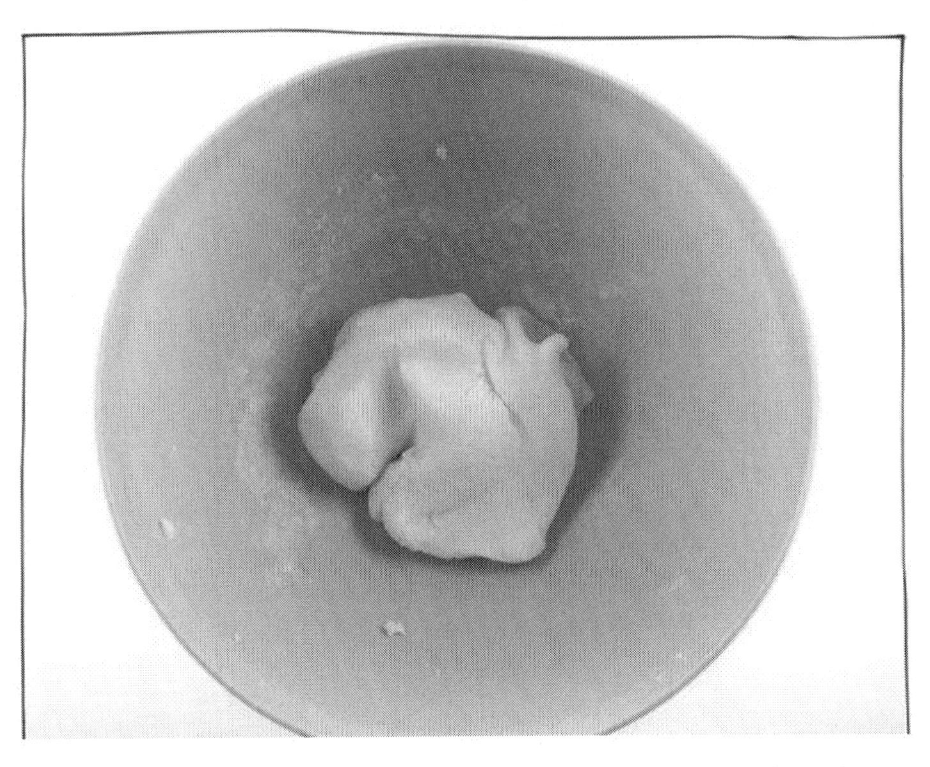

It may look very crumbly. Use your hands to gather up the mixture and form a ball. Knead it together a few times making sure everything is nicely incorporated, and the dough holds together nicely.

Take 1 tablespoon of the dough and shape into a patty. I like my vegan peppermint patties nice and thick, but if you are more of a thin mint type of person, feel free to make them thinner.

Lay the patties in a single layer on the parchment lined baking sheet. Repeat until you use up all the dough. Pop in the freezer for 15 minutes or longer to set.

Melt the chocolate chips in a double boiler.

Take one patty at a time and dip it into the chocolate, turning to evenly coat. Shake off excess chocolate then return the patty to the parchment lined baking sheet.

If the patties start to soften before you finish coating them all with chocolate, return to the freezer to chill as needed. Once finished and all of the patties are chocolate coated, pop the tray back in the freezer set for about 10 minutes until the chocolate is completely set. Enjoy!

Homemade Vegan Twix Bars

Looking for something fun to do with kids? Try these Homemade Vegan Twix Bars! Made with a buttery shortbread cookie, topped with gooey homemade caramel covered dark chocolate.

HOW TO MAKE VEGAN TWIX BARS AT HOME:

Prep Time: 45 mins

Cook Time: 50 mins

Total Time: 1 hour 35 mins

Yield: 16 INGREDIENTS

For Shortbread Cookie

½ cup refined coconut oil

1 tbsp granulated sugar

2 tbsp confectioner's sugar

½ tsp natural vanilla extract

1 cup all-purpose flour

Pinch salt

2 tbsp water

For the caramel

¼ cup canned, full fat coconut milk plus 2 tbsp

4 tbsp agave

3 tbsp organic corn syrup (such as Wholesome Sweeteners)

2 tbsp water

1 tbsp refined coconut oil

For the chocolate coating

1 cup vegan chocolate chips (such as Enjoy Life)

1 tbsp refined coconut oil

INSTRUCTIONS

To prepare the shortbread

Preheat over to 350F. Line an 8x8 baking pan with parchment paper

In a medium bowl, cream together coconut oil and granulated sugar for about one minute. Add confectioner's sugar and vanilla and continue beating for another minute, until creamy

Reduce speed, add flour, salt and water, and mix until just incorporated

Using your hands, pull the mix together to form a dough

Press the dough as evenly as possible onto the lined pan. Using a sharp knife, score it to form 8 even 1-inch strips, then score it once down the middle (you'll end up with 16 strips)

Bake at 350F for about 35-40 minutes or until lightly golden. Set aside to cool completely

To prepare the caramel

Combine ¼ cup coconut milk, agave, corn syrup, water, and 1 tbsp coconut oil in a saucepan. Cook over medium heat for 8-10 minutes, whisking often. Remove from heat, add 2 tbsp coconut milk and continue cooking for another 6-8 minutes, stirring frequently. Remove from heat and let cool at room temperature

To prepare the chocolate coating

Melt chocolate and coconut oil on a double boiler or in the microwave (20-second increments, stirring each time until completely melted). Transfer to a bowl wide enough to fit one of the cookie bars

To assemble the bars

Brake off the cookies once they have cooled completely. Place them on a baking sheet lined with parchment or wax paper

Spoon caramel over each cookie. Let them cool in the refrigerator for a few minutes

To cover with chocolate, place a caramel covered bar on a fork over the chocolate bowl. Dunk it in the melted chocolate, using a spoon to help cover the bar completely. Carefully shake the excess chocolate and return it to the lined baking sheet. Repeat the process with the remaining bars and refrigerate until the chocolate has hardened.

TIPS TO MAKE THE PERFECT VEGAN TWIX BARS:

Caramel will thicken and become chewier as it cools. If it becomes too hard to handle, just warm it up slightly.

It's important to let the cookies cool completely before assembling the bars, so the caramel stays on and doesn't run down the sides.

Use a good quality vegan chocolate to coat your vegan Twix bars. Use any chocolate or chocolate chip that you enjoy eating right out of the bag or wrapper.

NOTES

Caramel will thicken and become chewier as it cools. If it becomes too hard to handle, just warm it up slightly.

It's important to let the cookies cool completely before assembling the bars, so the caramel stays on and doesn't run down the sides

NUTRITION

Serving Size: 1 twix bar Calories: 215 Sugar: 16.6 Sodium: 3.5 Fat: 13.5 Saturated Fat: 10.3 Unsaturated Fat: .8 Trans Fat: 0 Carbohydrates: 23.5 Fiber: 2 Protein: 2 Cholesterol: 0

Strawberry Pate de Fruit

PREP TIME

5 minutes

COOK TIME

30 minutes

TOTAL TIME

35 minutes

Ingredients

1 pound frozen whole strawberries, defrosted

2 cups granulated sugar, divided use (plus extra for rolling)

2 tablespoons powdered pectin

Instructions

First, line a 9x5" bread loaf pan with parchment paper.

Place the defrosted strawberries in a blender, and puree until completely smooth, about 3 minutes. You should have 2 cups of puree.

Next, add the puree to a 2-quart saucepan, and clip a candy thermometer on the edge.

Whisk together 1 cup of the sugar with the pectin, and then pour this into the strawberry puree. (Pectin can clump if you don't blend it with the sugar first).

Turn the heat to medium-high, and cook the mixture, while

constantly stirring until it comes to a simmer, about 5 minutes.

Next, add the remaining cup of sugar to the pan, and continue to cook, while constantly stirring, until it reaches 235° F. Be patient, it will take at least 15-20 minutes, and it will seem to stay at 220° forever. Just keep stirring and letting it reduce.

Once the mixture comes to 235°, remove it from the heat, and pour it into the prepared pan.

Leave the pan at room temperature for 2-3 hours to set. I let mine set overnight, uncovered. If you live in a low humidity environment, you may want to cover it with plastic wrap.

Remove the pâte de fruit from the pan, and using a knife dipped in sugar, cut it into cubes. Roll each cube in extra sugar, and place on a plate to serve.